My name is...

In memory of my dear Gran whose words of wisdom I will always remember … "If you fall, make it part of the dance."

- KH

For Mum and Dad who have always lifted me up out of my worries no matter what.

- LR

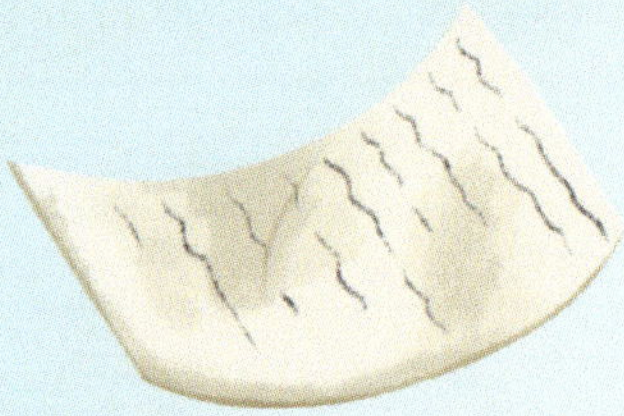

Layout and design by Lucy Rogers
www.lucyrogersillustration.com

ISBN 978-1-5272-7224-8

First published and printed in Great Britain 2020.

WRITE THE RIGHT STUFF

Karen Hart

Illustrated by
Lucy Rogers

There was once a young person called Blair.
Whose life appeared normal and fair.

Despite this, however, Blair
would often feel sad,
suffering from annoying
thoughts that felt bad.

Why was everyone cooler, smarter and better at sports?
Was it just Blair who had such negative thoughts?

A good friend suggested writing the worries down.
It was better by far than a constant frown.

That's what Blair did, but the worry pile **grew...**

It filled half the bedroom, *what was there to do?*

As the worries kept growing and spread even more.
It wasn't long before it reached the bedroom door.

In Blair's mind, to be cool, popular and to have lots of friends,
was all about having the right gear and keeping up with trends.
How sad that Blair thought this viewpoint was right,
lying awake worrying all through the night.

If only Blair knew other kids felt the same,
all trying to keep up with this *fake crazy game*...

Desperately wanting to be accepted,
but convinced that in time they'd be rejected.

Blair felt anxious and tense,

Nothing at all seemed to
make any sense.

Each night, the worry pile
just grew in size,

When daylight arrived, it loomed large in Blair's eyes.

Until some time later Blair's Gran came to stay, and said...

"Blair, come out, it's a beautiful day!"

Choosing however to stay in the room full of gloom,
Blair was ***trapped*** by the mountain of doom.

Gran came upstairs and opened the door,
"Look at this paper... I can't see the floor!"

Instantly, she gave Blair a cuddle
at the same time commenting on
the paper muddle.

"Let's make an immediate start."
And she walked to the mountain
as quick as a dart.

"These notes look like worry
notes, am I right?
They are feelings that bother
you both day and night?"

"Yes Gran, I write them down," Blair replied.

"That's fine, but don't let them pile up like this," Gran sighed.

"The point of writing things down is to see what's amiss."

With that she patted Blair's head and planted a kiss.

"Let's get to work and sort all this stuff out!"
She got on her knees and read each note of doubt.

Right, these can be thrown, because the
worries have gone,
and I think these are niggles that
didn't last long?

This pile are the thoughts that make up who you are.
Don't worry about those, they will help you go far!

They show you are thoughtful, decent and kind. Young people like that are a pleasure to find!"

"Remember Blair, some thing's we cannot change, this is life with no answers and I agree it is strange, people die both young and old, never forgotten by loved ones through stories told."

"So yes, Blair," said Gran, "Write your real worries down, decide which make you sad and cause you to frown. Then, take them to someone you feel you can trust, because sharing these thoughts is an absolute must!"

On hearing such wise words, Blair hugged Gran tight,
and felt sure now that everything would turn out right!"

Thanks to sensible Gran, Blair knew what to do.
That was to read the notes and review.

Those scary thoughts that could not be
dismissed, Blair now noted, and saved on a list.
These were the ones to be shared and discussed,
and hopefully sorted with very little fuss.

All the others however could just be forgotten!
Gran added, "At times, things will seem sad and rotten.
With you asking yourself why?
If it's night time, look up to the sky,

Find the ***bright north star.*** It will always be there
no matter where you are.

Remember also the blue sky may be hidden but is
constantly there. Grey clouds finally disperse and
move elsewhere.

There is always a way to work things out.
Even when you are full of doubt."

So that huge worry mountain was now small, flat and round, nothing more than a *tiny* mound!

It was such a relief! So few cares to discuss!

All the others had vanished with such little fuss.
Everything Gran had said gradually began to make sense.

Blair felt the anxiety lifting and felt far less tense.

Printed in Great Britain
by Amazon

47999966R00018